Dear Rev. John —
Thank~ for all of you love and
support, in poetry + otherwise!
Lari

Catalina

by Laurie Soriano

LUMMOX Press

ISBN 978-1-929878-87-1

First edition

LUMMOX Press
PO Box 5301
San Pedro, CA 90733
www.lummoxpress.com

Printed in the United States of America

Acknowledgments

The following people have supported me in my poetic life in various ways, and I would like to thank them:

Daniel Hoffman, Alan Williamson, Eloise Klein Healy, Amy Gerstler, Cecilia Woloch, Dorel Shannon, Alan Schwartz, Amy Blackman, Mark Nishita, Dinah Lenney, Jeff Duncan, Claudia Carasso, Dean MacKinnon, Abbe Lowell, Diane Faber, Naomi Guttman, Diane Warren, Julie Horton, Diane Hayden, Margaret Lazzari, Billy Steinberg, Dana Parish, Rev. John Morehouse, Rev. Kim Crawford Harvie, Alex Soriano, Eric Soriano, Chris Soriano, Andrea Moll, Chandelle Okumura, and Robert Douglas. Extra gratitude to Judy Werle, Cris Williamson and RD Armstrong for all their work in helping me realize this book.

Special thanks and love to my mother, JoAnn Englund, for always believing in me, as a poet and otherwise, and to my husband, Steve Rehaut, and my children, Lucas, Miranda and Grace, each of them for their loveliness and for being there in every imaginable way.

Poems in this manuscript first appeared in the following magazines:

"Betty's Dive" — *The Pennsylvania Gazette*
"Cross" — *West/Words*
"Coast" and "Early Birds" — *The Orange Room Review*
"Turtles" — *Gloom Cupboard*
"Spring" and "Looking Back" — *Heavy Bear*
"Roller Coaster" — *FutureCycle*
"To a Mourner" — *Flutter Poetry Journal*

Catalina

I Coast

II To Coast

III Being Here

continued >>>

>>> *continued*

IV Gazing Out

Catalina

Preface

Laurie Soriano became my music lawyer several years ago. I was sitting in her law office, for another reason altogether, and following some wild impulse, I leaned across the desk and asked her, point-blank: "And what do you write?" And she looked at me and said, "I write poetry." "Send me some," I said, and she did. And what a poet she is, by Heaven! She is a master of a particular punch at the end of all the lines, which she lays out perfectly, and then comes that uppercut, which slays you. She is a marvel to read, and it is my joy to brag on her every chance I get.

I really think poets are heroes, moving bravely past their fears – and ours, if you will – into places for which, often, there really are no words. It is out of that wordless source that poetry comes, as it must, as it will; for, as we know, the source of language itself is silence. It appears to me that Laurie moves in a fearless way into that silence, and that is a vulnerable thing, in and of itself. There, all exposed, she listens for what will come. In that place, things can come, and things can go. In order to get more, you have to accept loss, so it's risky business, this making of poetry. Yet, make it she does, diving down into the breathless deeps, climbing up on the high steel, risking everything in order to catch, then release, the gorgeous lines that fill up these pages. Made of individual moments, things close to her heart, her work speaks of the places where all life comes together. By holding up her reflective Self she catches these fleeting things, then turns the mirrored surface towards us, where, in the final measures, we see ourselves.

— *Cris Williamson*

Introduction

Fairfield, Connecticut, its dense woods full of secrets,
full of children with their heads ducked against the weather,
the wooded hills rolling down to the openness of the Long Island Sound,
whose mild waves have fled the raucous Atlantic.
Hordes of drunken gulls hover and skim,

dipping down into the grey waters. The breeze eventually pushes us
West, through the great rippling heartland, a bridge between Oceans—
we come hurtling out of the Rockies and speed through the desert,
finally opening our bleary eyes to the confident palms on the coast,
Palos Verdes, California, a peninsula puffing its chest out

against the Pacific; its striped cliffs telling the story of the mountain
that grew up out of the ocean, building itself with silt and lava, fighting off
the hungry ocean, becoming first an island, and then a proud figurehead
at the end of the land. Trees and humans perch atop it, unequal
to the glorious clash of land and water. Posses of brown pelicans patrol the coast,

plunging down 70 feet by the cliffs to pull
wriggling silver life from the froth. Facing us, 25 miles out is
Catalina Island, California, another mountain
that has built its way out of the water, another green land
beyond the end of the land. And she beckons:

Come further...

I Coast

Some Facts

It's raining snow away,
stubborn colors clenching in the mess,
neighbors' cars bright as flags.
My head aches from reading
in bed until noon. If you
care to know me, leave
my father's smoke,
the noise of us all hysterical
with Christmas. Run in a red sweatshirt
and wool hat, trudge the gravel up Congress Street
through the woods, feel the giddy
shift of ice. Crack the silence
with your footfalls. Be inevitability
with me down a hill.

Inventor

Believe plastic.
Take one of seven needle-sharp Ticonderogas.
Draw line. And line. Circle. Line. Now erase
the straggle-line. Draw the spiral. Draw
the spigot. There's the pump on paper.

There was a family joke: his head is in a pump.
The kids learned what *stare* meant when
he'd chomp bologna sandwiches, eyes two-dimension brown
as though his eyes could see their own circumferences
but they sort of looked at you.

If you asked him dad, how's a pump work?
He'd get out some gridded sheets, lay
eight Ticonderogas on the kitchen table,
and talk and sketch until you said the gang
is playing kickball, dad.

I don't care about your stupid pumps...
He heard that in your adolescent phase
when his spikes of vision pierced you. You'd try
to hug him, but his body was a block of lucite
until you whimpered dad dad I'm sorry.
Believe plastic.

Betty's Dive

I.
Later you remember. There was no rock
in the water, and the dive was perfect.

II.
Her laughing swells in huge concentrics as the others laugh.
She is a strong woman leading. Think of
shoulders twisting through a swimming stroke
while others follow floundering. Think of
splash fights in the water, and her cascades.
Of her scrambling up the cliff that banks
the river, snorting wit to all the dares,
shrugging off the mild warnings. Think of
(others having done exultant cannonballs)
a dive like none, those muscles twisting
as she twists her body through a flip. Think of
laughing when she does her dead man's float.
And then: c'mon Betty.

Tim Roach

A red-winged blackbird cries and rings
the pond, Tim Roach, as they drag
your muddied, bloodied corpse from
the warm water. Your face, bullet-shot,
is soft and smiling. The newspapers say
it was another drug deal gone bad.

You were a wordless nature boy; pet snakes
wrapped in flesh springs round your torso.
Your silent mother tugged you from the storm of
your father's house and drove you
to the bird sanctuary. In April,
when cars hit mama possums, raccoons,
squirrels, or when mama birds broke their wings,
there were blind babies gaping-mouthed
to be fed. You had the deftest fingers
of us child volunteers, could shove dog food
down bird throats with a bird beak's thrust,
could make those baby mammals
suck an eye dropper clean.

You were an ugly boy, ugly-named, but what
is the word for rapt concentration at a hawk
soaring spirals on October thermals?
You watched the wings move, noted special
tufts or stripes or beak, and, while we
riffled through our birdbooks,
said *osprey*, gave it its name.

No one could have cupped their hands around you,
stroked you, pumped you full of mama's milk
and then released you, ready to take your place
in the woods, the gentle captain of all animals.

Instead, you took the trail of destiny, battling
with your father, borrowing his sneer.
You shed your skin of shyness,
found girls (first, us girl volunteers),
found clouds of bliss (I heard the bottles
in your backpack, Tim),
and left the bird sanctuary.

To A Mourner

I watch you as you watch him in your memory:
walking wings for England in the First World War,
dancing in a grass skirt in the Philippines,
giddy-yap through Colorado, the last cowboy.

Then he was your father, swinging you by the hands,
dancing you in toddler's white shoes,
crooning cowboy ballads to his four-year-old sweetheart
when the collie died.
"Daddy knew how to fix everything."
Daddy did,

until the china head of your Bessie-doll
shattered into smithereens and daddy said
"I'm sorry babe," finally
scowling at the disbelieving tears
of his darling on his lap.

I cry as I watch you crying at the grave of my grandfather,
crouching like a child at the headstone,
saying daddy to a hunk of marble.

Dogs

Giving Minnie sitting lessons,
we think of other paws we've held.
This house is a menagerie
of shadows, but that is stubborn
human memory. We are tortured by
the echoes of dogs barking.

Dogs bark in single facts: need outside,
need meat, need a scratch on the snout,
need a reason to settle their haunches.
"Sit." Mickey sat. "Shoo!" Mickey left
the bedroom, sad about the uneaten
gerbils. We love this soul of dogs because
it blinks and obeys. We love our dog chasing
his tail, nails clicking on the linoleum floor.

When Mickey died, we cried because our work
was wasted, because we hadn't told him "Die."
While we mourned, Mickey relieved himself
of his old body outside, and wagged
in new greeting, a puppy hauled
out of a station wagon.

Parents

Our parents' teeth are yellow with corruption.
On trips in the car to grandma's house, they trapped
us with the insult of their smoking,
ordered the windows shut on account
of the cold truth of winter. Mornings
they'd hack away righteously in the bathroom
as their bodies strove to save themselves.
Pity our parents, for they thought it
harmless in their teens, even when they
coughed statements of black into handkerchieves.

Our long-suffering parents, with
their saddlebags and stomachs,
their plates mounded up with more cake,
more mashed potatoes. Their incomprehensible
butts, their padded everythings. We made
them park around the corner waiting for us
after school, not caring if they understood
why. They'd pull their blouses down, trousers up,
over their stomachs meeting the teacher, trying
to distract her with eye contact.

Then there was the drinking,
the reason we got hit
before bedtime, the reason we lay alone
shivering in our beds at unreasonable hours
hearing them murder each other, over and over,
leaving puddles of failure and self-pity
all over the living room.

Something—a photograph, an xray or someone
speaking too loud—froze them in the horror
of fat and old and uncontrolled.
Now they are pinched and afraid.
They went cold turkey off the cigarettes
and whiskey, and the fat is coming off
like birds molting. They've begun walking,
long strides in the morning sunshine,
their muscles laughing with surprise. The doctors
say they'll live forever.

Hit

It was dawn, and my brother knows the deer
are fey and simple in their running
when the dark sifts through with light.
He was slightly numb because he is,
and it was early. His road was

an accident interrupting the deer path.
He was going 40; the deer was
going 20. The car and the deer
were married in mortal injury,
but Chris was just fine.

He sat in the sand at the side of the road
and held the deer's head, looking
into its eyes. He tells me one way
to look at things is the deer was
other-worldly, looking away,

and there was no agony, no spite.
You think it's strange I have his photo
on my desk, when he was five, baby teeth
like a row of neat kernels, the smile of a baby
who must charm to survive. His cries

from being hit would tear through our
skeletons, because he was slow and
fuzzy sensitive, and the hitting
was more inane than death,
because here there was no peace.

Sister

My little sister's body carved itself out
this year, her legs got thin and shy,
like mine, her face took on the planes
and angles of our type of beauty, her hair
became a gleaming boast of abundance.

On this visit, she shares my bed
with me like little girls do,
and we murmur in the darkness
about men's bodies, our overlapping childhoods,
boring lovers, brutal ones. We
glide from inhibition toward sleep, and
whisper until we are closer than lovers.

The next day we lie on the beach and talk, pressed
down by the sun's hand. Our two long bodies,
thin and muscled, with our mother's capacity
in our hips. I see my sister's small pox
vaccination scar, remember the night when
she cried all night with the shot's little
spell of disease, the fat rosy exuberant
little doll all fussy and swollen. I close my eyes
and ride the waves of her woman's voice.

Turtles

Like them, I am dull, a raw, soft thing
in my hard shell, paddling about the tank.

We are all slow, the turtles and I, dragging
ourselves up on the rock to bask under the bright light.

See me stretch my neck luxuriantly,
my eyes blink alert, look at all

my pretty colors gleaming in this light
of yours. I launch myself back into

the cool water, necessarily, and bide
my time until I'm ready for more heat.

When You're In The Home

Have them call me in fifty years,
and I'll find the bed they've parked you in.

From the hallway, I'll know it's you carping
at the nurse because the game is over on tv

and you can't tolerate the crap that's
now come on. When you see me,

your eyes will blaze forth familiarly
and I'll make the mistake I always do

of thinking it's about me, when
it's daily life and womankind and

every particle of time that so enthrall
and torture you.   Still it will be

for me to catch that veiny hand as it
flutters through a gesture,

to hold that skittish bird, keep it warm
in my papery soft old woman's hands,

while you tell stories that somehow matter,
then settle back to take a nap.

The Sleepwatchers

There is one of two who sleeps.
The lady, not the minotaur.
The blooming mother, not the man
who talks to their unborn baby
and waits with his hands for its
kicks.
The mythic warrior come home,
not his weaving-weary wife.
Freud's wife.
The wrinkled farmer, still
radiant with sun.
And you, my warm enchanted one.

The minotaur always sits
stiff and watchful at her feet,
makes a right angle
with the body of the lady,
who takes comfort in her own arms.
I can hear him wait
while a clock
ticks
for sleep-words
like inkblots in the darkness.

Forces

scree

        scree

scree   me   scree

       scree

Kids nearby from Teaneck, music
on the ghetto blaster shouting
the waves away. They do this eerie
arms and legs dance to the music—
arms up legs up with the sax. And they
get up, move to the history of beaches.
The camera is the best befriended kid.
They flirt, like Arthur Murray has
taught them to dance the ocean,
like the girls' moms said,
don't let him touch your bathing suit.

I am like the

      s
    u u u   h.
   n n n   c
       a
     e
o c e a n b

the center or the circumscribing circle
of the seagulls. I am like
the spot on the blanket

between the two lengths of us
where our hands are knotted
as we talk with white eyelids shut.

There is a reason for lying
like a hedonist in-sucking sun,
after the body and the bathing suit
are their negatives—not the body,
not the bathing suit—
after the first pink twinges
after four o'clock ekes its old man's light
after the kids have headed back,
until there is this puffy mirror parody
until there is this farce of two sunburns
making love.

I remember the gulls; have them locked
like a jewel globe, their screes in three dimensions.

Path of Least Resistance

My mother will never forget the time
four summers ago when you were wearing
shorts. I knelt down by your legs
and like a salesman pointed out
the fine contours, the luxurious shadows
of your thigh muscles, the ropy
twists of your calves. *Look, Mom.*

The first time I took you running,
on a fine false spring day
in the dawn of everything, you did
a lap, then feeble calisthenics
on the astroturf while I glided
twenty times around the track. Maybe
just the spring air made me giddy.

When August was a dog with
its tongue hanging out, I'd
drag you out of bed and we'd
accomplish our five miles. Sometimes
I'd sprint ahead and loop back
to you, but your legs were like
machines now, like mine.

Four summers later, our love
floated to the ground, and I
took my hand from yours. I remember
the mild tears tripping from your eyes.
Then you had the first girl who'd
have you. Of course you stopped running.
Now on the phone you say you've always
admired my energy. I chuckle modestly.

Coast

The sound of the Sound is mild,
overwhelmed by the scree of seagulls
and children screaming in a sandy playground.
Parents set up chairs on the beach and gaze out
toward Long Island, or east
toward the raw Atlantic.

I never heard the Sound or saw it
those first eighteen years, even though it was always there;
never felt the great trees, breathed in the drug of Spring,
or even felt the ache of Autumn. There was
only the throbbing drama of a little house
on a road in the woods—a mass of children

building up like a bad headache, glints
of warm gold, all the good and bad human smells,
the awful never-ending swell of hope, the bruises
never given time to heal. And finally I was pushed
out, and looked down at my feet as they took one
step, and then the next, away.

II To Coast

Zeno's Paradox

Our momentum is the problem.
We dabble our toes in
the Pacific and ache for
shuttling further. All
we can do now is spin
mad circles, or cut back again.

The high school algebra teacher
smiles coquettishly: if you walk
toward that wall, halve
the distance, halve
and halve and halve
the distance, why, you'll
never ever reach the
wall. Class dismissed
and maybe three kids with glasses
staggered dazed in the hallway.

We have sliced a road, America
falling in neat pieces
to either side of the car.
We have hacked off our tail,
Connecticut, bloody and fresh;
the sting never stops remembering.
My mother, collect, long-distance,
says swallow the Pacific
and call me in the morning.
You'll forget.

In Indiana, we synchronize
our watches with the sun.
Even with a handicap
we swallow down like pills
that we will take three
crossings of the sun to cross,

three nights when my lover
and I remember each other
stealing twenty minutes on
the front seat of the car,
before we strap our seatbelts
on. I drive, he sleeps.

We are still at seventy,
I shift my cranky hips.
No one told us about
the mountains in Wyoming,
about farmland and stratified
stone, a horizon in
layers of history, men
and women scraping their hoes
and eroding, musing after supper.
There is redounding motion
in a porch swing swaying forty years.
They count fingers, not seeing their
horizon, knowing nothing else.
They would feel it
in their bones if a star
went out.

Later, she narrates
a cute corollary. Our hero
Achilles, the dream of our bodies,
as a youth has a ludicrous
race with a tortoise. The brutal
tortoise scrapes ahead. Our hero
sprinting muscles twanging
sweat in rivers nearly passes —
but the tortoise scrapes and scrapes.
Achilles' fate: a grizzled athlete
trapped within the paradox.

The air is cold and black

but my headlights
sort out a plane of bright
ahead. Three o'clock four thirty-five
I see there is a moment
where black has its questions,
a moment when the question's
answered: *day*, a moment when
a block of black becomes
a cow, just let out
in the stubble. Slightest stirrings
and I'm almost crying. Finally
I only crane for that
sweet old sun in the rear view mirror.

We are stunned by profundity
of stars here, can only say
can't believe
it can't believe it
which is all there really
is to say about those
straight sheaves of road,
that brazen cry of sage,
the sky hard and clear as words:
we've left. We're flying
through Nevada.

This is the saddest splash of water:
the Atlantic was dim and gentle
when we cried, clutching
our families on the beach.
We lost the moment, racing forward,
forgot their faces while
they were a foot away.
We are old at twenty-one.
Looked back and something
in us froze. Look
forward but our eyes never focus.

To Wallace Stevens: Climate

I know Connecticut winters, too,
know white inside to imitate
the snow too nicely. Bless
the woman, my mother, your wife, who
trudges in her boots to town for
the Times and some flowers wrapped in paper.

I have spent late-winter afternoons
fingering them in bowls, like a seer touching spring,
have through the window challenged stiff trees outside
to crude orgasms of flower. The bowl of carnations
was gone the next day, but I was outside gasping
in my sweater at almost-leaves
wrinkling out of twigs, invisible
flowers breathing on my neck—

But now it is a different winter. I am a woman,
have moved to California. I have learned
to buy flowers, change their water to keep it clear,
have learned that yesterday's carnations
smell their ripest in the dumpster outside as the children
frisk in the sun on the perfect lawn.

Venice After Work

The black dog loped round and
round the living room of the place
at Venice beach. Done chasing him,
she cast light on the white counters
of the kitchen, decorated for an instant
with gleaming brown jewels, which
were roaches, which were gone before
she grabbed a paper towel. She heard
the bored dog in the living room
let the moist tennis ball plop
to the carpet. Venice was

too many colors, the men selling
t-shirts, their voices tinted with unknown accents.
Even at dusk, graffiti overpowered the ocean.
They took walks before supper, solacing herself first
with the waves, of which he was in
cowering-to-the-sand terror. So they
looped back to the Strand for heading back.
She was grim and stately gripping his leash while he sniffed
strangers and urinated on the post
of a no dogs sign.
By now it was grainy dark.

My Birds

I am kicked out of sleep
every hour or so by the cops
in me, shouting obscenely that
the work's not being done.
My lover calms me,
and I bury myself
in the warm oblivion of his body.

I am knocked awake the final time;
the morning breathes through the blinds.
Birds are chuckling and singing
in the neighbor's tree. I lie
still and listen, exhorting the timid
birds in me to call back
to the birds outside. Sing
the sunlight, darlings. But my birds
are broken, their wings protrude bones.

My lover and I used to celebrate morning
a thousand ways. Now we spend our minutes
putting salve on my brokenness, nestling
what is good in our hands.

Watching Him Sleep

I watch him fall, impulses
strobing across his face,
forehead playing the accordion,
toes curling and going slack.

When the sleep words come, I talk
back, trying to make his soul grow
out of him like hair, but it breaks
and he falls back into shadow.

I must sleep touching him so
our bodies can commune
like horses in their stalls.
He gorges on sleep, his cheeks

puffing into flowers; I am
a skinny shy thing when it comes to sleep.
At breakfast, he surrenders his dreams,
and I study them like fragments of old bone.

Think of a rooster crowing
those normal notes, easy as eggs,
calling you back to the ground,
your eyes flutter, you are awake

in the country, and something is
frying downstairs. The alarm clock
is different, crashing its way across
my mind in a cruel instant, I see

colors that are dreams popping and
vanishing. My eyes spring open irrevocably.
He is unmoved, mutters about unfinished dreams,
and locks my jealous alertness in his dead arms.

Pathology

Your eyes are full of snow
and mine are raining
as I lie holding you
and wait for the medicine
to bring you back.

When the sediment settles
to the floor finally and I
can see clear through
to your thoughts now
orderly and quiet, I want

to tell you how I tried to find you
in your body, how your throat,
greased with pain, said things true
and irredeemable, and I
answered, patient and afraid

of your eyes like blazing coins—
your body would have killed me
in swift easy movements
had it meant relief.

Then I got you
the pills, and your muscles screamed
and went slack. I start to tell you
all of this, as you smile,

wan and helpless, tumbling
back among the pillows, and
I see the pain begin to flicker
once again behind your eyes.

To the Attacker

Let us assume my rage. I will
place it in a box and set it
on the table between us.

I was swollen with self-pity
that night. My car was humid
with the tears I was about to cry.
As you leapt into the car,
my head kept crashing through
layers of unreality. I almost
giggled with relief: the day's
welter of complexity was simply a dream;
I would wake up in the damp dark
in my husband's arms. Your gun was like
a toy—the invention of my uninformed
subconscious, but the air was clear and sharp.

Didn't you feel our intimacy—my body
and yours separate in the car, like lovers',
couldn't you feel how good and sad I was?
Those quiet seconds, you must have heard
my breaths coming fast, felt the heat
glowing out of my body. You hit me
the way a man hits a good for nothing
animal, your blows designed to knock
me out—I wasn't worth killing—
and dump me in the street.

Somehow, I overcame you—my goodness
or my punches laced with outrage
made you fall away.
I hunched over the steering wheel
trying to wake up as the car
filled up with tears.

You've slashed apart the ripe
abandon of my trust, torn away
the quietude I wore like a dress.
I am left with what is in the box.

Red Wine

Bloody liquid, he'd make me fill his glass
to brimming, so I was the child who nudged
him toward his self-centered stupor, caused
the electrical storm of his anger sizzling
and snapping. I saw my family bent and buckled
from his drinking and built a house of metal
for my bitterness.

My friends' warm hands, planted
on my elbows, steer me back
to the dormroom from the bar. My hands
grip the flesh of their waists as I stumble
further toward the land of my father,
the shifting land of regret and soggy laughter.
I awaken alone roiling and spinning
in the darkness on my narrow bed.

Holidays, daddy hunches over his decanter,
reaching out to pull one of us or another
into the bubble of his solipsism
for a shambling conversation. One day
I ask for a glass of wine, and he pours
it with a glad drunken slosh. I nurse it,
trailing after him, *daddy come back here*
and we will walk together. Soon he
devolves into hiccups in the bathroom
as I fall into my childhood bed,
my head pounding colors.

In a restaurant, I am thirty, and
I ask daddy if we want wine. He fills
our glasses like love, daddy never loved me
like wine, and we start thinning our blood
with this red stuff, our words flow
like liquid, we laugh fit to bust, and
we walk home arm in arm,
like we never did.

The next night he fills some glasses
so they dome with surface tension.
No, I say, too late. *Maybe we should
take it easy.* He smiles lewdly. I am
the deflowered virgin saying no,
a blameless orphan destined for
a life of crime.

Crash

It was before summer dark
when lawns are lush with secrets
and the sky hums with romance.
Two separate vectors of light and sound,
the effect of all our causes,
you and I shuttled separately to the spot

where our masses would marry
and your blood would stain the street.
For a moment, one of those *out of time*,
we hung in the air, as breathless as sweethearts,
before we came together, your motorcycle
tearing a path through my car,
as your body flew
three car-lengths forward.

The next was a scene from a movie,
shot slow with strobes. Me moving
from the car swimming through the twilight,
your body lying long and quiet, me starting to run

toward a house for help, starting to run
to take you in my arms, until
I was reeling awake at your feet,
my head in my hands. A man ran up
and swept me aside like a curtain
to minister to your greater need.

The witnesses took form out of the darkness
and held me by the elbows, it's not your fault,
it's not your fault, while other words
kept bubbling out of my mouth
and everyone smiled patiently, hoping
the shock would wear off. I perched

on the firetruck seat holding a Kleenex from the cop
for the tears that wouldn't come
until they wouldn't stop. And I yearned
for your brokenness, to fit the pieces
with my hands, to take your head
from its helmet, and kiss the plastered hair,

but you were cordoned off, officials gathered
like frowning fathers around you,
and I was left with the lawyers
who put my words for you on paper
and burned it.

Dogs II

Another old lady among her flowers
snips and rakes, pulls and stakes,
closes her eyes for a second
to smile in the sun. Next to her,
an old dog stands by, dacchsund mix,
alert and ready, her fat stomach
grazing the ground. They are basking
in the same strip of sunlight.

When we'd all given up on grandma,
when she'd turned into more
cancer than woman, she held on
for two more years. We all
avoided calling her, confounded
by her stubborn slow marathon dance
with pain. As we thought about
her furniture and bonds,
grandma's voice squeaked out of the bedclothes,

and only Lady kept listening,
her whitened head tilted in attention,
her long, low body poised to help.
Grandma used to slap that dog just
for being alive, but Lady
with her nervous desperate love
licked the bitter hand as it pulled away.
On New Year's Day, when grandma's body

finally was pried out of the bed,
all that remained was Lady,
lying by the bed moaning – a low, dark howl
that gripped our stomachs.
Someone dragged the dog outside
and tied her up in the Kansas winter night.

Tonight I drive home rippling with stress,
my eyes strain to leave their sockets.
Mikey waits in the yard, absorbing the darkness
in his dark fur. When I touch his head,
I am brought back to my body,
hair and bones and itches, and I roll
my face in the darkness and sniff. I will
lose my sense of smell, I will lose
touch with my fingers, I will moan for days
when this creature dies.

Home

Home is in my mother's voice; can you hear
her calling me down for breakfast,
warm-voiced and pliant, while dust careened
through attic sunbeams? She always distilled sweetness
in her voice and applied it to my forehead like a cool cloth,
even when a million fires must have raged in her.

When grandma died last year, my mother and I
shared a bed and talked in the haze of drowsiness.
I was floating in her voice even as she spoke
of being now an orphan at the age of fifty-six,
of how her own mother, unemotional and strong,
ushered her through childhood in Kansas, how
she tripped along the railroad tracks home from school,
to be hugged by a cardboard body.

Now her voice, across long distance,
is sweet on my forehead on my birthday
as she speaks of shouting at the doctor
Are you sure? Are you sure? when he said
she'd had a girl. And daddy drove her back
through the Connecticut leaves, with the sky
hysterical blue, as my mother brought me home.

Cross

Some start as young boys,
yearning for the safety of their sisters'
dresses. It's easier to cry in a dress,
rocks are rarely thrown at you,
aged uncles spare you their pornography.

Some are born cross-dressed.
Wilde to Hemingway, their mothers gussied them
up like girls, their hair grew in obscene
pipe curls, with bows, they wore adorable
frocks. Until their hair was shorn,
until they pulled their knickers on,
they were soft and sweet and dreamy,
their mothers' dolls, safe
from their vicious fathers.

You sashayed into the living room
wearing your sister's crinoline, did
a little curtsy, you were six or seven.
For a moment, the colors swirled around
you as you waited for your parents'
laughter. Instead, your father jerked
you by the arm and clumsily pounded your
backside, then shook you, glaring into
your eyes, his anger flecked with fear.

You played every sport, won the scars
and broken bones of well-adjusted
boyhood. They dragged you out of
dusky corners where you'd sneak
your books, shoved you out to co-ed
parties, shunned any boy who took
too much time with you on the phone.
Despite it all, you emerged loving women.

I want to dress you up in beauty,
build you a cocoon of silk and feathers,
block out every sound of violence.
You're a little boy before the First Step
away from your sisters. Be a flower.
Let your skin be little boy soft.
Let your hair fall loose and easy.
Remember how to cry.

Poem for our Wedding

I love you the simplest words,
your pure colors, your clear
cry of pain. I love you
the pink humming
of the sky at Venice beach at night
and leaning back as we walk
to wash our faces in the air.
I love you the shaggy
smiles of dogs and the brilliant
attention of babies.
I love you singing,
I love you sweating.
I love you the relative
truth of our bodies,
the basic rule of our compassion,
the perfect, unreachable
beauty of your eyes.

III Being Here

Lullaby

Can you hear me? As I hum
the song, I tumble
back upon its waves. My mother
murmured it with her hands upon the mountain
I made of her abdomen, and here I am
encircling you with water and with primal sound.

Sometimes, if my voice cracks in anguish,
or I curse at a driver, or I sob
in the restroom as self-pity
wrings me out, you feel the tremors
surging through my body, crossing
the placenta. I cannot spare you this.

I want to sort life in neat bundles
for you, label them, but already details have
scattered, whole sections
have blown away. When I die,
you will find the story full of
holes: I refused to pose for photographs;
I tore pages from my journals
in a fury; they are landfill now,
with the world's eggshells and diapers.
The past was a dog with my
blood on its teeth, the future
was a hungry dog. Having run
myself skinny and tired,
I meet you now with only
a few trinkets in my pockets.

When I saw your fins and tail,
your heart fluttering
like a tireless bird on the screen
of the ultrasound, when I felt
you sloshing patiently, whirling
in the waters my body'd made,
I discerned the music I heard
before remembering, floating
into the moment and out,
all directions the same.
We will each of us float there again,
but I am not afraid.
I will teach you many things
I promise, but remember,
you taught me the first thing.

Spring

Leaves are whispering down, my people
shipping out in moving vans and caskets.
My fingers are listless against
the white sky as the rain begins, and
birds fly twirling and laughing
from wire to steely twig.

The earth has tipped, some I loved
fell off and some rolled elsewhere.
As the moving trucks trembled to go forward,
we kissed briefly, our bodies separate,
and leaned our heads back to keep
the tears from spilling. I have learned
the stolid set of my face when unobserved
when I am gazing off beyond the distance.

The trees revel in the sky
stark but radiant, shaking
off the last of the rain
as a child cries off in the distance

and I go inside and up
the stairs to comfort him.
As he slackens with sleep,
my own murmurs melt me,
my warm fingers on his forehead,
and his unburdened breathing,
and leaves are sprouting.

Expecting In California

These little eruptions in my abdomen
are of my deepest knowledge but
unexpected, and my hands are greedy
resting there, waiting for more bumps.
Soon the baby's mass will ripple
my flesh and start to hurt me
at the wrong angles sometimes.

My friend stands on the cliff
for hours watching the infinite weave
of the ocean for a snag when finally
the whale surfaces for air
or flips its tail, and I see
the barest flash of froth
as it goes under and she points wildly,

but I have no need for this, for nature
has enough of me now, and I'm sleeping,
perhaps the baby's kicking even now
as the bed shudders and the earthquake
wrests me up and I am running fully awake
as though all other moments were a fraud
because this wasn't happening.

Later, the languid aftershocks, with my hand
on my belly as my own tremors work,
and I float helplessly, the thinnest membrane
between this child and its earth.

Florence

They've locked her eyes shut with Krazy Glue,
and the powders and rouges have brought
the pride back to her cheekbones,

her stillness is natural. We've identified
the body, and the coffin lid closes—all this artifice
for God? The rabbi speaks gently

in the rain about a life whose single value was
endurance, father handed her to husband
with a dowry of violence, and her soul

flickered out. She barely touched
her only child, spent years in her apartment gazing
out the window until they let her move

into the Home, then thirty years healthy,
hiding, until finally the disease
ravished her and carried her off.

I clutch her great granddaughter
under the buffeting canopy
among the stooped shoulders of this tribe.

Stories

"Dream of me when you die," you say
at bedtime, and I catch my breath,
gripping your solid little shoulders.

We speak often of my death, like a party
or a trip I prepare you for, only I'm not
dying soon that I know of. You want the rhythms

of our rituals, yes, you'll be
an old man, and I'll be ancient and tired. But
that doesn't answer it. You refuse to be deterred

and I'm a liar for trying. You talk
of your dying first, and I laugh it away.
You make me promise not to put you in a box.

My teeth are wearing down already, everywhere
gravity, entropy are doing their work.
This is all the more exquisite

as your limbs telescope out, your skin
sweet, unrusted yet by hormones,
but there's a shadow on your brow.

After the surgery, when I held
your angry, writhing limbs, you moaned
coming out of the gassy darkness I let them

send you to, you bellowed at the cruelty,
and I tricked you again with the reassuring warmth
of my hands. Five years ago,

the clouds at sunset had angels in them,
and I called you down. Someday I'll be up
in the pink mist waiting, dreaming of you.

Swimming Pool With Child

A painting of blue and light—
white circles dappling the wall of the pool,
the sun tossing coins on the water's surface,
the water's aqua giggling at the bolder sky,

and a child swims the length of it, not yet four,
sturdy legs fluttering like that's all God made them for,
eyes wide behind goggles. As she swims to me,
her mouth stretches back in a certain grin,

and I am waiting for her underwater, grinning back.
The picture's complete as I receive her in my arms,
skin to skin in the deepening blue shot through with light
and sweep her up into the sweet air.

Testament

Our daughter's voice floats up from the reaches of the minivan—
"when I was a teenager, before I was a baby...,"
this normal chatter about her life before we gave
her life, and now from her car seat, she's telling you
about her job, her job as a . . . and in your mind
as clear as the stars tonight, you see it,
and she says precisely what you're seeing,

and you are not surprised, husband,
you who believe in nothing but the dull substance
of your flesh. When you tell me the story,
I laugh, unkindly dispelling the magic,
and grab it for myself when you're not looking.

Our son has testifed about life in the womb—
"I remember bloody red flowers"—
and I don't breathe as I ask
"what else?...what else?..."
and the bubble of memory breaks.

When each of them was handed to us,
grey-black eyes dazzled and dazzling,
we would vie for the warm bundle,
face peeking out from the tight swaddles,
and stare into the eyes
and little else has ever mattered.

My Boy

The crack of a bat, and your torquing body
made it, and somehow nine years ago
my body made yours. Your cheeks
are streaked with manly pink,

and those blue eyes, which can glint
with the magic I've sprinkled in, those blue eyes
are dull steel, all about nothing
but finding the ball with the bat
and switching its fate.

The laws of manhood let you slide—
actually teach you how to tuck
the one leg back, project the other
toward the base, breaking all my rules
about those precious limbs.

And what about stealing? You do it
even when the coach cringes, you take
base after base, humiliating the other boys
when they drop the ball. Finally,

you thunder home. Your face softens as
you touch my fingers back through the dugout fence,
but soon you turn with an absent smile
and sit and squint, studying the field.

Fresh Meat

Each time I tried to slay them
my monsters got bigger,
grew longer teeth. I run myself skinny
back and forth over the same fields
craning backward to gauge
their paralyzing progress.

How suddenly they vacated
my dreams. Now I stroll
nightly through empty
chewed up pastures.
That motley flea-bitten crowd has found
its way to you, my tender son,

now you've a man's body, your mind
pink with possibilities.
Sleep is a dank village
where their roiling hordes abound.

When the night demands you
finally you submit,
your body taut in your bed,
a forearm sharply guarding your face.

Those beasts blast in,
demanding attention at the bar
They jump and spit and riot,
shaking the foundations
of our peaceful place.
I drag you gray and battered into morning.

I would throw myself before
any beast, offer my flesh for yours
without a flicker. But as you start to run
the gnashing mob grins and brushes past me,
rejecting my stale comfortable blood,
raising their heads to sniff for fresh meat.

Mourning Mother

Woman, hide your face, so the rest of us
can shimmy our hips, dancing in the sun,
and push our wriggling babies out
into the hands of the world. Your rivers
have ruined the land, still radiant
but broken. A mother cannot bear
what you have borne, singing last lullabies
to your child, watching his forehead unwrinkle as he
floats away from life. Yet here you are,
ashamed of your survival, nursing your secret
darkness, slightly tipping your face up to the light.

Daughter

Please, never grab a cactus like that
again—even plants can't be trusted.

Still, you've given me these hours I've
memorized each countour of each finger,

extracting bristle after bristle from
your warm skin, and your hand,

sore and sad, belongs to me too.
Your arm has gone slack with trust.

Impatiens

That night I came home
and told you I'd met a man
whose face was like a flower.
You and I sat at our little student table
eating dinner, our bare feet
lightly stacked together like

one person's four feet.
A moment of your blue eyes
glancing off my green, before you nodded.
What did I mean by that, and how did
you know without asking?

The man is simple like the earth, loamy, radiant
and when my eyes behold his face,
the confident smooth masculine skin gives way
to the flashes of color that no one deserves
that are his eyes, flashing that way
because of me.

The pots and beds in our yard are full
of happy flowers, smiling crowds of pink,
giggling gangs of red, bright orange,
white ones with pink hearts. They are
nothing if not patient with my sporadic care,
although I love them always. Called impatiens
because they give their seeds away
without a moment's doubt.

Of course I left you within weeks of meeting him;
you and me split apart was like surgery on
Siamese twins. I'm sorry for the bloody agony,
and all the years it took for your organs to take hold
on their own. We could study him together, you and I,
celebrate and analyze without understanding one whit
the flower of his face. The three children

that he gave me have little flower faces
I often cannot bear to behold, and
my life is enough.

Grace

Your little hands wear a line
of callous from the monkey bars.
Although you're five, I still own
your body, like the mama ape
hunting for fleas on the little one,

but now you've made this hard ridge
on your baby hands. You swung from bar
to bar, often skipping one, your face
vivid with the effort, as though nothing
matters more than qualifying as a monkey,

and I caught you as you dangled from
the last bar, and I was glad. When we
intruded and found you dreaming in
my womb, they told me even before
I'd thought of it there was an absence

of protrusion, and that meant your body
was building all of those beautiful pipes
and holding chambers. I can't tell you
how to be a girl, and you're
not asking. I curve my body around yours,

stroking the callous as I hold your warm hand
as we read, that straight white body
with its confident slit, those easy muscles,
and your eyes spilling over with careless flowers
are only about teaching your mind the words

so you can swing away.

The Way There

You grab my hand from the back seat to the front,
your face a too-white ivory,
your violet-blue eyes go deep and dark
as your breath catches, and your father takes us
through another curve. You gape
at the drop to the Valledichiana below,
curve after curve, the shoulder
of the road mere millimeters,
and you finally start whimpering.

When I was your age, we'd
cross the giant bridges over the Hudson
going to New Jersey in the VW bus,
sometimes even in great gusty storms.
I would stare down at the black chop
of the river, and at the modest railings
at the side of the bridge, and suck in my breath
and usually clamp my eyes tight

as I'm now begging you to do.
I tell you how strong and sure
your father is and how
safe we are, but I close my eyes too
even as I murmur and grip your small hand.
I finger through my memories of when
fear became the truth, of how I'd
stagger around the newly broken landscape
until it seemed natural and full of new colors.

Once your father and I closed our eyes
and held our breath, and there
you were, fat, pink and healthy
notwithstanding your and my ordeal,
and your father held you in his muscled arms
and first bathed you in his voice. Now we've arrived
at our house on the cragged hill in Italy,
look at the world we can see from up here.

Sweet Bean

My nerves are jangled when
the bright black hair sprouts brashly
on the smooth skin of the modest bit of you
that, beneath the diapers,
made you the first little girl.
The peaceful nipples wake up and announce
pinkly *the parade of hormones is here*,
the breasts bloom into little pillows,
your belly flattens, the waist carves itself,
and suddenly you have a colt's legs,
big feet, and a supple back that someone
ought to paint a picture of.

I find you stretched out in bed, a nude
on pillows. I tuck your sadness
in among the blankets, stroke your forehead, satisfied
because I knew I'd find you here like this, your skin
pleased with your ripe tears, and
because my hand and voice can make
the morning sun make diamonds
on the wet grass, you smiling with tears.

Hands of Women

I.

Let my body move you down into her hands in latex gloves
helping you work your way out after you've crowned,
now a sharp shoulder, now your slippery midsection, and then
the rest of you in a wet glad swoosh.

They are doctor hands veined with science but woman soft
and those firm hands will catch you, she'll hold
you to her ribs as the cord is addressed and then lift you up
and swing you to my chest, and then I have you,

Hello baby, hello you baby girl, and you peer at me,
squinting, and we share a silent joke (me through tears),
before I tuck you to my breast, and you
competently do what is needed

as I feel her hands below, delivering the afterbirth,
then tending to my birth wounds before
she pulls the gloves off with a snap, then
jots statistics on a board.

II.

I offer my sad cracked back to her.
First her hands only listen, persuade my body
to tell where it's crying, and then with her steel muscles
she orders it to *breathe*

as the candles flicker, and in this dim room
a voice chants *Ashanti Ashanti*, and my face
is being ground down into the cradle
as my back unclenches, and sighs.

Sometimes we talk, as she kneads a shoulder, a calf,
my face directed anonymously toward the floor, voice raspy
as with no one but a lover, skin warm
and wanton, hair a wild mop. She delivers me

back to the world all slippery and smiling
and I float home, where I find your teenaged self
reading curled up on the couch, and I slide next
to you and take your hand lightly in mine.

Etching

First you coat a piece of smooth copper with wax.
Using a needle, squinting, you scratch the shape of a grackle
through the wax, submerge the metal in a bath of acid,
which eats away at the violated copper. In two hours

a shiny plate emerges from the bath with the bird
etched upon it. You slick the plate with ink, wipe, then
place it in a printing press, run damp paper through the rollers,
and the grackle rolls out, dewy and startled with its life.

Pulling away from our hug, sister,
I notice the surprised lines that pain
has carved around your eyes, the fire
blazed up from your hips through the

branches of your spine, leaving twiglike
scorches at your temples. You and your suffering
own one another like the metal and your needle,
the damp paper and the ink.

Tangerines

Pluck one, and the branch yields it forth,
touch the peel, and it falls away, the sections
ease apart. The fruit in your mouth is fresh
and easy, a brief tang to the roof before
you are suffused with sweet sunshine.

Somehow the universe handed us the keys
to this house of liquid light and wood,
with its garden, awash in wanton flowers,
plants luscious with the green satisfaction
of growing a few hundred yards from the ocean.

And the trees—pines, palms, oranges,
lemons intertwined with bougainvillea,
peaches, and the tree with the green hard
fruit that suddenly glowed orange in December
and softened up—we thought it might be

tangerine. Christmas morning, dad
woke up and saw the gleaming clusters of fruit
among the leaves outside the guestroom window
before he strode out obligingly to sit by the gifts
with the grandkids, waiting for the grownups to stumble in—

so unlike dad; when he was only our dad,
in our little brown Connecticut Cape,
we'd always had to beg and then negotiate
that morning, please please let us wake you
at eight, praying he wouldn't spew his normal
poison and ruin another year. He never

raised his voice that whole Christmas here;
who'd have known that cancer
had him by the lungs, not even he, and
by April, he was tossed aside,
stone cold without cooling off,

and the tangerines hung there waiting
that whole visit, we didn't know those
ornaments hung down from the tree
ripe and ready for him, a mouthful of bliss
for that dying grey man on a visit
from the Cold, because we didn't know
our trees yet, so new were we in this blessed house.

Roller Coaster

So sorry for all the times I refused your hand,
that pushy life of the party hand that wanted
to guide a daughter across the dance floor.

Kansas in August, our faces clammy with old sweat.
Standing in line for the Mamba, I surveyed the crowd,
everyone younger than you by twenty years,

as you chatted sociably with everyone
and me, my friend at last, even as your rotting breath
foretold next April's joke upon us.

The slow clicking climb shifting to the cruel drop,
and you laughed "holy shit!" (just as when I clutched
your arm and the organ started thundering my wedding march).

You turned to check on me, and you took the long curves
with gritted teeth, silent and steady, ready to grab
my hand if I needed it.

Bless you for daring me to ride the Mamba,
and for my screaming like a child, echoing
my joy and fear all over Kansas.

Forgive me, father, that I only held your hand
when the I.V. ran through it
and your life rewound behind your eyes.

Charlie's Widow

You cupped your hands so tight
to save the dank water of his life,
but it slipped through your fingers fast,
leaving them dry in seconds, and you
wetted them with bright tears.

You are reeling back and back,
now he is alive and young,
those black eyes hot as stars, and
his hands so sure and urgent,
the voice flowing, making music
on the rocks, and you flowed
with all of it, always,

like when your mother stood
in the hallway in her housedress,
her head in her hands, as you packed
your things, your face on fire
from his kisses, and she pleaded that you wait,
think, and you almost laughed out loud!

and there was his Indian motorcycle
humming by the curb
and those hips waiting for you
to surround them, and your mother
at the window was a flash of sorrow
as the two of you hurtled up the street,

only now he has fled by himself,
that swaggering street kid, and you
have started to smile and shake your head,
remembering the ride, forty-seven years
before he let you off, slipping away
with nary a wave, and now you put your hands
tenderly to your own cheeks.

Priestess

Wipes the spit away, swabs off shit,
reveres the sweet oil
of your skin. Nothing that your body does,
nothing that your mind does is foul.

She sits at your feet,
massages them, washes, as
she gazes up sidelong to your face
to read its fluttering for meaning.

She lowers her head, surprised that
she allows you to splatter her with rage or
worse, that she admires your shifting furies like
the swirling patterns of the weather.

At night, she curls herself around you,
walks the rutted road of your breath,
searching along the way for your baby self,
the teenaged, the old man you'll be.

Mornings you sing rawly,
and she hears the notes without
the hanging moss, she collects your words
like so many muddy nuggets of gold.

Cat

A black cat sprinted onto the freeway
last night, and the thud of her life
going silent was just like any old piece
of road trash taking another lick,
but I'd seen her ignorant fear,
as the light made her eyes haunting moons.
This animal was playing the odds
with no chance, and it was I who made that true.
Not one strand of fur was left on my tires
by the time I was home inspecting them in the dark,

and I leaned, crying into the metal of the car,
rejecting the cold glamour of the stars,
taking one shuddering inhale—
when I smelled that the orange trees
had put out their blossoms,
the frank night air doused with sweetness,
and my body smiled, taking the rest of me
with it into the sleeping house.

As the light breathed back into the bedroom,
I dragged my body, unrefreshed, out of bed,
but he murmured to come back.
In the morning he is a monument
to all that is good about sleep,
simple clouds of forgetting, and
his shoulders going miles around.
The warm bulk of their muscles
soothed me, and all I was is the cold
awake bones melting in his arms.

Instructions

Bread

Flour water oil salt.
Give the yeast what it needs,
learn the warm elastic satisfaction
of the dough when it's ready
and coddle it again, cover with a clean cloth
and leave it somewhere dark and safe.

Plant

Never give up on an African violet,
even when it withers and protests
that life is too long and hard.
Feed it, give it mist and comfort,
soon the crooked fists will cock upward
and open into the same startling flowers
you've seen there twenty times before.

Trash

Believe it or not, it is your job
to build a garden on top of the landfill;
see that sea of garbage? When you are done,
it will be the underpinnings of the most luscious Eden,
strap yourself into the backhoe and start folding
the trash under.

Girl

Give her milk and sunlight.
Keep her clean, hold her hand—
even when it's soiled.
Help her laugh her way out of anger.
Let her eyes polish themselves. Sit back
in the audience and watch her up on stage,
dreamy smile as her body invents
the song she is dancing to.

Rabbit

She is an armful of luxury, only she has
the right to wear her rabbit fur coat.
She detests your hands caressing her fur,
but her life somehow depends upon it. Regret when
she is caged for safety.   Let worry wander
the house with her when she's free.   Leave her
in the yard in a pen to hop in the freshening air, but
never ignore the shadows of hawks on the grass.

Dog

Pluck her from the desperate cityscape, she has nearly
disappeared in the vicious sun, no food, no water, nothing
but matted fur, a chain around the neck,
memory centers of the brain that are crammed
with cruelty. No amount of comfort can quell her trembling,
but *try*. Bathe her in ease, and when hatred
explodes from her throat, do nothing
but pity her.

Birds

Suffer with the yes and no of their cages. Hide
around the corner as they warm to their themes
each morning; you depend upon
their symphony. Roll them outside when it's fine
so they can build their repertoire beyond the squeaks of cabinets
and cellphones. Let them compare notes with the wild birds.
Roll them back inside as the sun wheels out over the ocean.

Woman

You gave the bread its air, its earth.
The plant breathes for you, and you breathe back.
The child and the dog both cleave to you,
the other animals are vivid in their circumscription,
and yet they all lift their heads and watch you as you
round your way into the room. The grace in you
is the grace in them.

In the Event of Failure…

No such thing, if you love them all.
Don't be ashamed of the aged, the damaged.
When something perishes, find a clean box
of the right size, and bury it in a blessed place.
Let matter become matter.

IV Gazing Out

Catalina

My island is *the pure one*, Catalina.
I would lose myself in the endless churning ocean
were it not for this recumbent beauty sprawled
across my piece of the Pacific. Some days

she is not there—in her place is rose mist
or pale bands of smog out above the water;
some days she is a layer among cut-out layers
of cloud, but I recognize her outline—

the curving hills, the slim waist
at the middle where Twin Harbors is.
Last night it rained hard without warning,
the earth violently insisting on itself.

This morning Catalina is a statement in greenish black—
the ancient rock, the modern trees as bright as flags,
like she can answer everything.
She is where to go next, where not to go.

Fireflies

Let's open the jar and let them fly away
before it's too late. If we're lucky
the fireflies will thrust their dusky bodies
into the darkness, and then off in the distance
they'll send back to us an affirmation of
yellow light. All that I ever had of you

has crumbled, perhaps because my hands held on
too fervently. My mind still catalogs
and highlights, has built an archive
of baubles and stories, but all I have left
in my hands is the phone with your voice
flowing out sometimes like clear water.

This morning the Island is awash in baby blue
and pink, the stars still glitter, and the ocean
is a bowl of miracles. I run into the scene,
thus changing it, have left behind the dream of
painting the impossible loveliness of it all.
Looking down at my running feet on the path,

I jump over each snail dragging itself meaningfully
from one side to the other, I honor each little
sculpted life. When I look up again,
the sky has changed one subtle shade, and
I imagine you are flying free out
past the line of the horizon, glinting.

Jacaranda

As May in LA dances
drunkenly into June,
your clouds of zany purple flowers

appear suddenly, scream for attention
among the orderly ficuses and palms
along the great boulevards,

slam into the senses, make me
sing without notice,
force me to put on
summer dresses, showing skin

then gradually your hilarity drops
in peaked purple heaps on the sidewalks,
and you revert to the sober green of summer.

I am driven mad by waiting
for next year's purple, by wishing
to be satisfied with green.

How

how every scene composes itself, the more wild
the more exquisite, as though a hand confidently
scattered the seeds just so, balanced the purple bushes on the lower left
with the mist of yellow weeds on the upper right running infinitely to the sky

how the spheres pipe music into the twilit hospice room
as the man draped in coarse blankets wheezes out
his last days in delirium, sweeping open a lucid window
of an hour to sit holding hands with his brother, as the nurses come and go, silently

how the nurses draw the drapes, and the same music echoes as the mother's body
takes a steady drink of petocin, hour by hour slowly
relenting to yield the baby up, and the mother's mind drifts in
and out, as the barefoot doula rubs her feet with oil

how the master of the universe bows his powerful head
and begs forgiveness of the court, while a strong arm
grips his shoulders tight and later guides him out
the courthouse door toward the dimly lit future

how each morning I bring the beta back to life,
watch the dead mass unfurl into a fluttering flower as she makes ready
to dive up for the pinch of brown flakes that I administer
to keep her floating in her small amount of water on this earth

how the newborn, her eyes burning lasers into
her mother's eyes, knows to suck using
every muscle of her face, instructs each breast
to make the gift of milk the baby needs

Early Birds

I.

They are hollow-boned, take their clawed hands
and guide them gently to the car, rolling the little suitcase
so light it must be filled with feathers.
Her hair is a puff of white, his a scattering of dry grass.
They bicker still, chirp/cheep in harmony,
nothing ever clarified, nothing really matters.

Tired from the flight, they totter off to bed;
if you peek in, you will see their bodies side by side,
done with hormones, the precious ragged breath lifting their chests,
heads barely denting the down pillows. In the earliest of morning
they are perched on their kitchen chairs with the newspapers,
the day already swinging full when you rise...

II.

It is getting to be time now. When you get
the phone call, or perhaps you will be
in the hospital room when his or her breath
flutters to silence, open up your arms
in a gesture both of letting go
and embracing. In the weeks that follow

keep your eye out for a sparrow hopping
and twittering a bit too close, a lark
that seems to be smiling on a branch nearby
and then shows off flying for you.

Parrot

Chewing his tongue, bobbing
his head the way she did,
it's not that the parrot is grandma,
exactly, bold slashes of color
so carelessly borne, those eyes
little domes of knowledge and waiting.
Birds were grandma's poetry:

She'd putter about the kitchen,
ever more deaf and silent, but she heard
as they muttered in their cages,
patiently cracking nuts, examining seeds,
and she would answer: "Pretty bird,
pretty bird," withered hands reaching in
to touch the bright feathers.

Stroking his beak through the bars,
I know that I must buy him,
because of grandma, just possibly
she has sifted back in, and in my kitchen
the claws will clutch the perch,
the eyes will bulge with urgent secrets,
and maybe he will sing.

Concert

A mockingbird lives in that tall dead tree,
holds forth mornings about the nature of sounds
and vice versa. I share him with my visiting sister,
along with the orange trees, all my affirming animals

indoors and out, and the hum of silence here.
She lingers in bed each spring morning
for a week, borrows our mother's ears,
parses the mockingbird's morning talk show

into its borrowed calls—a gull, a bug, a crow.
My parrot Albert in his cage is wheeled outside
for sun and the scent of orange blossoms
and to trade notes with the mockingbird.

They trill and whir back and forth—
a cell phone ringing, a snatch of me singing,
a cricket chirp as birdsong.
My sister hears their interplay

and her voice crying out
its bravo is our mother's voice.

Blessed Woman

They ran off together in a messy riot of sweet mud
and new flowers, and the two of them were
alone forever after on this loamy earth,
we children a product of their passion, and then chased off.

Our mother sang lullabies to our father through the night
before the cancer took him, and we all gathered round
as she kissed his forehead before they closed the casket,
the final act of a terrible, perfect love.

As a widow, she soared and crashed, took off again and flew straight,
sang dirges and celebrations, invented the life that
a woman could have alone in a warm house in winter.
We children swarmed about her, incredulous that she was free, and ours.

Fifty years after she was taken by passion, it
happened again, with the same force, her body
and mind racing ahead of each other toward
the Spring meadow that is love. She put forth

pink blooms, so much more lovely
on a weathered tree.   Now we are voices
from another realm, a breeze she hears sometimes
sifting through the tender, brilliant leaves.

Death of a Stranger

Noon baked the parking structure roof as
Mary clicked open her car's locks, getting ready

to slide into her place, like the man who clicked
open the neighboring car. He stumbled,

danced a little drunken polka, fell to his knees
as Mary, throwing aside the careful menu of her day,

went to him, studied his fading face
as he sank down to the pavement.

She dialed 911, then took hold of him, at first gripping
gently as though honoring the heart attack

that wracked him, her arms a delicate net
around his shoulders, her fingers cool on his skin. He went

heavy in her arms as vitality sifted
out of him like sand shimmying down

the waist of an hourglass.
Now her grip lost its civility, cinched tight

as her warming body made every loving argument
for staying on this earth. She felt him shift

from more alive to more dead than alive,
then finally all dead, and she gently laid him

down as emergency workers swarmed out from the stairwell,
too late. She sat crumpled on a curb,

as the universe swiveled grandly all around her,
and she stared down at her useless arms.

Backyard - California

"Count what was bitter and kept you awake." — *Paul Celan*

The lemons proliferate, grow ripe to yellow
finally giving up and going brown on the cement,

waiting in vain for lips, teeth, and tender tongue.
The palm tree asks me to hug it, its trunk

round and clean, wants me to lay my face
against the iron bark. Once I gaze up its length

to the yellow rays slashing down, then avert my eyes,
sink to my knees and breathe the tree's heart

until the sun rolls on its way.
Count the lemons with cups of sugar,

count gallons of dark water with
stars winking in the bucket. Count me

sleeping softly under the palm
counting lemons, counting stars.

Let Down

The clouds' bellies bulge, nearly bursting
with elixir the land so begs for, the mouth
of every animal, vegetable, mineral open in a big O
below, waiting for a drop of water.

Let down. Let it down. Let gravity
feel it has accomplished things today.
Let down, the hills by the ocean are brown
as the waves laugh below.

Trees and cats, boulders and mailboxes,
everything is dusty and dull, waiting for
its color back, our lips crack, the rain
will solve everything, while

the baby waits, her mother so pinched
around her fear, the baby's eyes have locked on
to the mother's like magnets,
the baby's mouth roots to the breast,

which safeguards the milk within
its secret sinuses; finally the mother
realizes she is resting
in the hand of a great giant, helpless,

and she closes her eyes and surrenders,
lets herself down, lets it all down
and with the let down
the milk starts to flow, and the baby

settles close in and
gulps with her powerful jaws
as the mother feels grace curling in tendrils
over both of them, as outside

it rains and rains improbably, and pelicans and eagles
row down the coast, diving
to gorge on the fish bristling in the freshening
waves, the hills gone mad with green.

Lapse

I.

They've streamed through his life
babyhood to dotage, and he's petted, fed,

litter boxed, gripped leashes, briskly dug holes
for their carcasses. Now his rumpled lap is vacant

as he works a puzzle calmly, and the cat
without any bidding slinks up in a sure black leap

to this soft but structured place,
and family members come and go

around the grizzled man encircling the cat,
until he starts to rise, and the cat and then the lap

disappear, and he takes himself to scrape
the white stubble from his face, not

wondering why this is necessary
because the cat has gone to her bowls

and is neatly lapping water. At night,
she chooses him—his light bones, his unassuming warmth,

and he lets her curl close or separate until she leaves for a prowl
out through the French doors into the sea of ink.

II.

The morning mist retracts to show a black medallion on the street,
she is curled in on herself like at the beginning,

and all of the yowling for meat, all of the lap sitting,
all of the pawing and pouncing is done,

she is nothing but bloody fur and cat bones
circled in on themselves, and the family

sleep restlessly until the old man rises and shuffles out
to the driveway for the paper and gazes toward the street.

Later, his daughter vacuums the furniture
to remove the last precious fluffs of fur,

the children chatter of a kitten,
and in his bed, in shadows, the unshaven

dilapidated old man weeps.

Gravity

Since he was a boy, he'd always
had loose ankles like a marionette's

and consequently learned to fall—keep
your head up, fold torso, unlock

elbows, drop your palms to the ground.
Once, when he'd been running miles and miles,

a rock floated up and tripped him,
the machinery of his chugging legs clanged

to a halt and he crumbled to knees and elbows,
ripping off flaps of flesh, but his body

responsibly rose and recommenced its
steady chug toward home, forehead

gleaming in the late sun, blood streaming
down his sweaty calves and forearms.

His body is a picture book of all the tumbles
he rolled through and now

so many falls later, his colors
have faded to white, he can't hear

can't make himself heard, and doesn't even mind.
Last night punch drunk dream dizzy

he smiled/tottered/fell, allowed
his head to make first contact with the floor tile,

cracked his cranium so that blood began to soak
the centers of his brain like the red blossoms of the womb.

Is it called falling
when you surrender

to the planet's pull,
forego stark verticality for

the chance to lie still
against the earth's warm chest?

Gone

Barbara used to say without
a sunroof she'd perish,
she needed the birds to hear and be heard,
needed to gulp air in fresh mouthfuls.

She sang out in flutish confidence
when the cancer cells lay randomly
sleeping in her endometrial lining,
her eyes were slashes of sapphire

distinguishing every gray landscape,
but her voice later caught on snags of doubt
as her womb welcomed the disease.
Still she strafed the beach for trash,

poured compost on her garden in autumn
after tucking in her bulbs
for the California winter.
As the daffodils' green fingers

dug their way through
the luscious loam toward light,
she began to lock herself
away, perhaps to shield us

innocents from the sight of
her other organs submitting obscenely.
I left vibrant offerings of flowers by the door,
by the next day they were always gone.

One summer morning as the birds
performed the opposite of a dirge
she siphoned up and out
an open window, her pain left

folded up on the bed,
the rest of her a pile
of dry rose petals
gladly falling to dust.

Bay

The swells gargle great mouthfuls
of the black rocks, then spit them
back tumbling ever rounder on the shore,
the way words lose their edges
as they roll mumbled from a mouth.

Do you wish my great lesson
for you were more than:
Let's perch on the bluff
and consider the air, water, birds, rocks
as each minute assembles a new universe?

I wish for nothing more than
the angles at which you hold
your camera, your raw young fingers,
the thousands of shots you take
of the impossible bay and later erase.

I have invented nothing
nor even ever graduated beyond
the gulls, nor they me, I appreciate
the swagger they take from their bright uniforms,
they appreciate my French fry.

Looking Back

If we leave the windows open,
we can hear the sound of the Pacific
crashing every night. In the summers,
we are serenaded by sea lions—
a song of lust and dominion
ringing out among the dim rocks.

We have come to a screeching halt
at the edge of the continent,
like cartoon characters clinging
to the edge of a cliff with bare feet.
We ache for shuttling further, for
the oblivion of the new.

A trail of tears leads back across
the land to the vigorous Atlantic,
a trail we need to follow to make
our peace at gravesites, to celebrate
the anguished earth, to piece back together
with tender hands all that we have broken.

Gazing Out

Running on the lip between what is real
and what else there is, as the waves
of the Pacific crash hungrily below,
I am balanced on the razor edge

of the continent, taking in all
the blue possibilities as I move.
Today languorous Catalina lies propped
on an elbow and dreamily gazes back.

I see the lighthouse ahead up the coast,
its light pulsing faithfully, while a full moon
lays extravagant silver on the ocean,
outshining the competent early morning sun.

These dependable legs
round through their cycle,
arms swing with joyous efficiency,
the lungs ask no thanks as they puff out

for the one billion, eight hundred ninety-
eight million, four hundred sixty seven
thousand, two hundredth time. How many
jumps, stumbles, bumps has this body

weathered, how many strokes through water,
how many hours of the writhing ecstasy
of love, how many years of work to build
three babies, then feed and tend them?

And still I roll along above the ocean,
ready to leap or fly, until my body turns
to climb a hill and finally, obediently,
takes me home.

Photo by Lucas Rehaut

LAURIE SORIANO lives in Palos Verdes, California. She attended the University of Pennsylvania, where she studied English in the College of Arts and Sciences and studied marketing in the Wharton School of Business; while at Penn, Laurie studied poetry at the undergraduate and MFA levels. She received a law degree from the University of California, Davis, where she also participated in MFA workshops. Laurie is now a music attorney in Los Angeles, representing recording artists, songwriters and others in the music industry. She is married to Steve Rehaut and has three children—Lucas, Miranda and Grace, and current pets Lulu, Albert and Chico.

http://lauriesoriano.com

ABOUT THE LUMMOX PRESS

LUMMOX Press was created in 1994 by RD Armstrong. It began as a self-publishing/DIY imprint for poetry by RD. Several chapbooks were published and in late 1995 Lummox began publishing the Lummox Journal, a monthly small/underground press lit-arts mag. Available primarily by subscription, the LJ continued its exploration of the "creative process" until its demise as a print mag in 2006. It was hailed as one of the best monthlies in the small press by John Berbrich and Todd Moore.

In 1998, Lummox began publishing the Little Red Book series, and continues to do so today. To date there are some 60 titles in the series and a collection of poems from the first decade of the series has been published under the title, The Long Way Home (2009); it's a great way to explore the series.

Together with Chris Yeseta (Layout and Art Direction since 1997), RD continues to publish books that are both striking in their looks as well as their content...published because of the merit of the work, not the fame of the author. That's why there are so many first full-length collections in the roster (look for the *).

The following books are available directly from the Lummox Press via its website: www.lummoxpress.com or at Lummox c/o PO Box 5301 San Pedro, CA 90733. There are also E-Book (PDF) versions of most titles available. Most of these titles are available through other book sellers online, as well.

The Wren Notebook by Rick Smith (2000)

Last Call: The Legacy of Charles Bukowski
      edited by RD Armstrong (2004)

On/Off the Beaten Path by RD Armstrong (2008)

Fire and Rain—Selected Poems 1993-2007 Volumes 1 & 2
      by RD Armstrong (2008)*

El Pagano and Other Twisted Tales by RD Armstrong
    (short stories—2008)*

New and Selected Poems by John Yamrus (2009)

The Riddle of the Wooden Gun by Todd Moore (2009)

Sea Trails by Pris Campbell (2009)

Down This Crooked Road—Modern Poetry from the Road Less
    Traveled edited by RD Armstrong and William Taylor, Jr. (2009)

The Long Way Home edited by RD Armstrong (2009)

Drive By by John Bennett (2010)

Modest Aspirations by Gerald Locklin & Beth Wilson (2010)

Steel Valley by Michael Adams (2010)*

Hard Landing by Rick Smith (2010)

A Love Letter to Darwin by Jane Crown (2010)*

E/OR—Living Amongst the Mangled by RD Armstrong (2010)

Ginger, Lily & Sweet Fire by H. Lamar Thomas (2010)*

Whose Cries Are Not Music by Linda Benninghoff (2011)*

Dog Whistle Politics by Michael Paul (2011)*

What Looks Like an Elephant by Edward Nudleman (2011)*

Working the Wreckage of the American Poem edited by
    RD Armstrong (2011)

Living Among the Mangled (revised) by RD Armstrong,
    special edition, (2011)

The Accidental Navigator by Henry Denander (2011)

Catalina by Laurie Soriano (2011)*